Am I OK—
If I Feel
the Way I Do?

AM I OK—
IF
I FEEL THE WAY
I DO?

Sr. VINCENZA
GAGLIOSTRO
S.S.N.D.

NAZARETH BOOKS
Doubleday & Company, Inc.
Garden City, New York
1981

ISBN: 0-385-17437-3
Library of Congress Catalog Card Number: 80-2077
Copyright © 1981 by The Catholic Heritage Press, Inc.
Printed in the United States of America
First Edition

To Sister Virginia Sebert, S.S.N.D.

Contents

Acknowledgments

I wish to thank in a special way Shalom Weaver and Richard Gearda, former graduates of Holy Name School, Providence, Rhode Island, who helped with ideas and outline of the book; Mr. Jay S. Sweeney; and Mrs. Margaret Oryell for her hours spent in typing.

Thanks to Doubleday & Company, Inc. for permission to quote from *Looking Back* by Joyce Maynard.

Introduction

An attempt has been made in this book to answer some of the questions you might be groping with. You may agree or disagree with what I have to say. This is your privilege. My hope is that you will come away with one idea, one thought that will make you proud of who you are. The only thing I want to say in this book is that you should just be *you*.

One thing we have in common is that we need each other. I need you to bring out the love that my generation may have buried. You need the love that we adults can share. You are our future. You are our hope.

This book comes from my heart, and it was written to encourage you to be yourself in a world that is hungering for someone like you to reach out, to dispel misery and sadness. It challenges you to shed your teen-age hang-ups in order to be someone special. Someone who has the character and the ability and desire to choose right from wrong.

I know what you're thinking. You're right. You will find it a difficult task. You will sometimes be criticized or teased. It takes a lot of guts to be what you really want to be. It's much easier to be what your friends and others around you want you to be. So when I ask you to get rid of your teen-age hang-ups, I mean I want you to shed your fear of what others are going to say. You may never be free from fear, but at least when you are trying to be you, you can put your fear on a shelf somewhere and act as if you were not afraid. You will find that once you shed your hang-ups, you will really belong. You may even find yourself one of the leaders.

I am challenging you to take up where my generation has left off. I am challenging you to take risks, knowing you might be mocked, to make your world and this world a better place. You're going to be mocked! I guarantee you, there may be many "mock outs." Are you willing to accept that, or are you going to climb into a shell and say, "Well, this is what the gang wants me to be, so I don't want to make any waves"?

I am challenging you to make waves. I'm not encouraging you to be a rabble-rouser, but I want you to be a person who stands on your own two feet. I'd like you to be someone with a backbone—not a jellyfish.

What I have to say to you in this book is what I feel. I hope you can find one sentence that you agree with. I hope that something I write makes something you do or something you believe make more sense. I hope that something you read will help you to be who you really want to be—who you really are.

I want to hit home. When I do, I want you to stop. Take time to reread. Try to figure out how you can use what you read today! You might even have a special friend, a pastor, a teacher, or a parent with whom you can share what you read and what you think about it. Do so!

One thing we have in common is knowing that we need each other in a world in which we can feel isolated and deprived of human caring. I think that young people today are not feeling loved. So here is what I am saying to you: I love you so much that I want to challenge you so that you are willing to risk being hurt. I want to challenge you to get out there and do something. Don't sit back with your "light under a bushel basket." I value you.

I do not see you merely as young people growing up who will soon have to face adulthood. I see you, as I would like you to see yourselves, as a special part of this society.

Many of us are looking forward to meeting the real you. We want to love the unique you, and we will appreciate it if you will just do one thing: be you and not what others want you to be, for only in being yourself will you have peace of mind.

In Hebrew, *shalom* or "peace" means completeness or well-being. Peace is the state of mind that comes about when our lives are in harmony with God's love. Our Lord's prayers often spoke of peace. He told us that this peace he offered was his gift that he wished for us. My friends, I ask what you want out of life. Hopefully, you want to be at peace with yourself, and you want to be one with Christ, who is our peace. I pray that you will gain new insights about yourself as you read on and that you will realize what a gift you are to society and how much you have to offer. I also want you to think about "letting go"—of hang-ups, fears, negative feelings. Let go and be free to be yourself for others in your own unique way. The time has come for you to be, to grow, to share—most of all, you are OK if you feel the way you do.

—Sister Vincenza

1. Me, Myself, and I

Being Young

I am challenging you to be who you are. This requires that you accept yourself even though accepting yourself can be unpleasant at times. Do you have moments when you don't like yourself? Many times I don't like myself. At times I feel I'm a witch. Some days I wake up and I'm horrible. But I have to accept myself that way, too. However I am, I am always me. I have to accept myself in all my moods and with all my needs. We have horrible moods, and we have good moods.

Some days you can awaken and say, "Boy, I'm fantastic!" On days like this, when you have that good feeling of accepting yourself, you feel free. Suddenly you have good feelings about your friends and your family. You like everybody. You don't feel any bitterness, any resentment, any jealousy. On days when you accept yourself, you know all you've got and you know who you are. You can look at yourself in a mirror. You have nothing to hide. You know what you like and what you dislike. You don't have to be afraid. You can simply say, "Yes, this is me. There are no more secrets. Nobody knows any more about me than I do. I am really free."

Lots of people talk about freedom and liberation. I have discovered that, for me, there is only one way that I can be free or liberated, and that is to accept myself—the whole package: my weaknesses, my strengths, my ugliness, and my beauty. When I can finally accept myself, no one can do anything to hurt me because of who I am.

You can arrive at that kind of acceptance, too, but you have to do it for yourself. No one else can do it for you. No gang, no friend, no teacher, no pastor, no one but you. I can talk to you and tell you how great you are until I'm blue in the face. But if you don't realize it somewhere inside of yourself you're never going to feel it. That feeling of freedom has to come from inside. And that freedom will come from you, and then the real you will begin to step out. I want the real you to step out. Come out here. Stand up and be counted. I challenge you to this.

Being Alone

"Me, Myself, and I." When I look at the title of this chapter, a contemporary song comes to mind. Remember "Alone Again, Naturally"? It was about a man who was jilted by his girl. He found himself lonely and rejected, and he began to feel sorry for himself and feel that life wasn't worthwhile. Did you ever find yourself alone at home or at school? How did you feel? Were you afraid? Did you feel rejected by your family and your friends? Did you feel that life was not worth living?

Let's pull away and get into a mood of aloneness. Make believe you're the only one at home. Your mom and dad went out, and your sister and brother are out with their friends. Go to your room and lie down on your bed. Don't play any music; just leave the glow of your bedside lamp on you. Well—creepy, right? Are you afraid? If you are afraid, it's OK. It's a natural feeling. It's healthy, provided that you try to find out why you're afraid to be with your best friend. One you can totally trust. Did you ever think of yourself as being your own best friend? Maybe you are afraid of what you'll find out about yourself. But how bad can you be? What horror could you possibly find? If you think about it for a while, I promise a surprise. You'll find out that you're not so bad. You may even be better than you imagined. You just have to give yourself time to know yourself.

It takes many of us years to feel good about ourselves. Yet, if you really work at it, it may take some of you much less time to begin to get this good feeling. It's a shame that many people have to wait so long for it—perhaps until their thirties or forties.

But feeling good about ourselves is also a lifelong process. You'll never be able to say you know yourself completely because you will always be growing, and growing means changing. Each month, each year, you will be different, and then you will have to learn to accept that different you.

Looking at Yourself

Just ask yourself these questions: Who am I? What am I doing here? Why am I in this particular family, school, and town? Who am I to myself? Let's try to discover together just who is me, myself, and I.

Are you game? If you are, let's not waste time. Did you ever stop to think why you're stuck with your family? Why you're stuck with the same sister and brother? A father who drinks, or a mother who never cares and she's out all the time? Did you ever think that maybe they do love you? That maybe they need to find this love from you first? You might have to be the first one to give your hand and say, "I do love you, even though I don't like what's around me. I belong to you. We can stick together."

Or do you find yourself in a nice family? You love your father and your mother, your brothers and sisters. You feel so good about them. Yet you take everything for granted. You just sit around, never offer your hand. But sometimes they're looking for that hand. They're looking for a little bit of love. A little thank you once in a while.

Do you have a mirror handy? Stop reading and get one. Look at it now. What do you see? Don't laugh or frown. It's you. Take a good look. If you look closely, you may catch the twinkle in your eye. They always tell me I have the devil in mine. I love it. Do you have pimples? We all have pimples sometimes. I still have pimples. Nothing to be ashamed of. It's part of your maturity. It's part of changes in life. You don't need to hide them. Just wear them and be you. The real you. Not the one that others want you to be.

Every morning you have to face yourself in the mirror before anyone else gets to look at you. Can you look at yourself and say, "I'm not too bad after all"? I hope so.

Do you ever have trouble figuring out your feelings? Like one minute you're happy and ten minutes later you're sad? Feelings are an important part of who you are, but they are not the whole of you. There is more to you and me than the way we feel. We have personality and talents, and only God knows how much is endowed in each of us. Part of what our lives should be about is the continuous discovery of our potential and our God-given talents. We are called by God's love to develop our potential and our talents. We are called to be to others what we are to ourselves, but first we have to be ourselves.

Feelings as Signals

Feelings are something that you just can't deal with overnight because you change from minute to minute. Feelings have a way of telling us how we feel right now, not how we are going to feel next week or next year. We cannot honestly say, "Next week I'm going to feel happy."

Feelings are our signals. They are signals of our behavior and why we act the way we do at different times of the day. Sometimes the way we feel is a physical response, other times it's emotional. We need to be attentive to our feelings so they can help us learn to be ourselves. Even more than living day by day, I suggest you live moment by moment. Moment by moment is much easier than, "Oh, my God. I have to go through the whole day like this."

You will see as you get your life together that you'll be able to live according to the things you find valuable. Put your act together. Try to decide what is valuable to you. Who is important to you? What are your values? Where do you stand? Where are your principles in life? If you can put all of that into focus, you will have your act together. No one can come and shake you because you know exactly where you are. At least for today.

But you can't live your life based on feelings alone. You have an intellect, a body, and a spirit that also completes the picture. It is important to be aware of your feelings, and it is equally important to know that you don't have to act them out. If you're angry at someone you can merely say to that person, "I'm angry." You don't have to punch anyone in the nose.

Your feelings are not separate from your body, your mind, or your spirit. All three of them work together. If you're not well physically, you will tend to have a lousy personality that day. Your thinking will probably be warped. If you have a good day and you feel good, you're going to be happy and clearheaded.

Sometimes I feel better as soon as I say to myself that I'm not feeling well. I realize that I'm not an awful person, I'm just not feeling well, and I can't cope as well at that moment. In other words, if you face things, you won't need to fight yourself. Sometimes there's a problem because you want to do what other people expect of you. But you can simply let go. You can let go of a feeling of sickness by just saying that it exists, that even though it can affect you, it can't control your life.

Are you someone who tries not to show it when you feel miserable? Even when you're feeling badly, do people think of you as a happy-go-lucky person? Do you ever feel that you just can't be miserable that day because those around you want you to be happy-go-lucky? Then what happens? You go through a trauma inside.

Let go and be yourself; let others see that you don't feel good. Don't overdo it, but give yourself a break.

If you want to be a person of strong convictions and values, then you have to make decisions. But feelings affect all our decisions. In order to act well on your feelings, you first have to have a good, healthy self-image. All of you have an image of yourself. How you handle your feelings says a lot about what and who is valuable to you and who you really are.

Crying

By the way, do you cry now and then, or is such a thing not acceptable to your peers? You know, a good cry is a sign that you are a person, man or woman, who has deep feelings to express, whether joy or sadness.

How many of you saw the TV movie "Son-Rise"? It was about a three-year-old boy who was autistic— withdrawn in a world of his own. His parents and sisters spent hours working with him to help him make contact with the world. I don't know about you, but I found myself crying all during the movie. The love of this family and their courage overwhelmed me.

How about the movie "Something Special for Joey"? It was a true story of a very sick boy. His older brother gave him his Heisman trophy, the highest football award, because Joey showed great courage in fighting leukemia. How many of you guys mocked him because he cried openly when he made the announcement dedicating his trophy to Joey? I met a man who was there when those awards were given. He said the sobs were unbelievable from all the men in that room: the press, the athletes, the owner—unbidden tears.

The point I'm trying to bring out is, don't be afraid to be human. Don't be afraid to be the person you want to be. Remember, you have to look at yourself every morning in the mirror before others do. See yourself with curlers, braces, or pimples— and smile and face yourself and others.

Letting Go

"Letting go" is an important part of dealing with feelings. Think about the following example. You and your friend have gone through school together. You have spent eight summers together, and you have all these dreams and you talk and you listen to each other. Your friend leaves in September and comes back after six months having been exposed to a whole lot of new people. Different interests have set in. You're still friends, but your interests and experiences are not the same. This is what you have to deal with. There's a change, and neither of you is acting the way you used to.

What are you going to do about it? Are you going to go into a slump? Or are you going to accept that maybe you both have other interests now and still be grateful that your friend came back to you? Take your friend as your friend is today. You cannot keep things as they were and keep your friend, too. Now your friend has been exposed to other things where you haven't. So here's that growth process—letting go of a friend to keep a friend.

I think that's true with adult friendships. When you have to leave, you don't really want to leave your friend because you have something good going. But sometimes, within that leaving, you can allow a space where that friend can grow. There is also the problem of not wanting to let go of the friend because you're afraid you'll not make another friend, or that you'll lose this one. But you will probably find out that you don't lose. The mere fact that the person came back means you did not lose them.

Sometimes you do lose friends, but this is one of the risks you have to take in life if you are going to get the full benefit of relationships. This is why I stress the whole idea of letting go. If that friend is your true friend, she or he will come back to you no matter what. If it's meant to be that your friend is going to find other interests and other friends and not come back, you can still look at the good times you shared. You were important in that time. Don't think that all the years you did things together were for nothing.

Don't be possessive of friends. Give them room to be themselves, so you will have room to be yourself. Let your circle of friends be wider. You can always have one special friend for confidential things. It's good to have a special friend to talk to about girl friends and boyfriends, or about problems with your parents or school. But the idea of letting go is essential. Are you willing to let go? Do you know yourself well enough to let go, or are you hanging on to your friend?

Keep some time for yourself to be alone. Give your friends time to be alone and with others. That time is good and healthy. It provides opportunities for reflecting and seeing if you do have a friendship. When that friend comes back and things are not the same, is the friend different, or are you different? Letting go helps you face the fact that the person has come back and is no longer your friend. This is very painful. Are you willing to say, "Well, that was that"? Most likely, you're going to feel your whole life is shot.

Things like this happen early in life, usually in junior high or high school, because friends start leaving. You might even become afraid to make friends again, afraid to form ties because you don't want to be hurt. But remember, the moments in life shared between friends are really important. Some friendships are only meant to be temporary, based on such circumstances as going to school together or working together. Not every friendship is what we call a permanent friendship. We need different people at different stages in our lives.

I went back to my hometown after twenty-three years. There was a boy I used to walk home from school with every day, and he came back to visit me. It was like we never left each other. Unbelievable. Of course, our interests had changed. Our whole life-styles were different. I'm a nun. He's married, has children, has a beautiful wife. Yet that friendship is still there. We were able to sit down comfortably and take up where we left off twenty-three years ago.

Friendships are important. Parting is hard. Tomorrow's unknown can be frightening. We need each other. Still, we can misuse people. This is why, when I talk about me, myself, and I, I'm thinking about the idea of maintaining honesty within ourselves. For only then can we begin to be honest with each other.

2. Do You Like Yourself?

Liking You

Do you like yourself? I don't know why exactly, but many of us have to work hard to learn to like ourselves. Yet I will guarantee that, as you begin to like yourself, people are going to begin to like you.

Have you ever stopped to think that, just as you look to others for approval and example, they might be doing the same with you? What do you have to offer? The bully self or the real self?

The image we reflect is based a lot on our experiences. If we've had it hard and we dwell on it then we'll have others feeling sorry for us. We don't want this. We want others to look to us most of all for having character.

When we have problems, do we handle them or fold up and sob and play the game of How I Feel Sorry for Myself? "Look, everyone, here I am! I hate myself. The whole world is closing in on me."

You are at a time in your life when the challenges coming your way might help you to find within yourself that special strength or power that could enable you to rise above the problems that confront you. You have all this within you.

If you say to yourself (and believe it) that you're

not so bad, that you're really nice, people are going to start thinking, and maybe even saying, "You know, you're not bad. You're really nice."

What you project is what you're going to get back. If you don't love yourself, neither will anybody else. And I mean love yourself. Not a big ego, but love. Place value on yourself and your accomplishments, whatever they are; learn to have respect for yourself.

Respecting You

Do you take care of how you look, or do you enjoy being sloppy? Trying to take care of your hair, keeping clean, using deodorant or perfume or cologne, all of these actions say something about you. They make the statement that you have an awareness that you are special and that you want to project yourself as being special. You can make yourself feel good by being clean and neat. Your body is important. Your body is as much a part of you as are your mind, your spirit, and your emotions. Keeping your body clean and fit is part of a healthy outlook. You see, if you don't think of yourself in a special way, don't expect your friends to think of you that way either. That's what it boils down to. If you think you're important, so will others, and they'll come to respect what you have to say and what you have to offer.

The truth is, we don't want anyone to feel sorry for us, for after a while friends get sick of "feeling sorry," and they expect you to get over whatever problems you were facing. You might think you want your friends to be there to take care of you if you have a bad day, but I don't think you want that. If you care about yourself and others, you can simply say that you've had a rotten day, but you're getting through it, you can carry on, and that's OK for today.

Knowing You

You get what you give. You give bad vibrations about yourself, that's what you get back. You have a right to know what you want and feel. If you constantly try to figure out what others think you ought to be, you'll never have a chance to be you, and you may never be happy or at peace. Stop asking what others want of you, and start looking into yourself. You are not the center of the universe, but you are important. Look into yourself, not to the point of being depressed, but to discover the fine points in yourself. You have so many abilities. You have a lot of power within you that can enable you to do things without needing help from other people.

This is a time when you can prove to your parents that you are able to take on responsibility without folding. Why do you think your parents think you're immature? It is often because you fold on little things. You may shed tears like a water faucet. And you pretend not to care about anything.

Instead, you might offer to help with something,

or own up to something you did. If your father asks who broke something can you say, "Yeah, I broke it" and take the consequences? Often, when you're honest with people, they'll be honest with you. When you are honest, you don't hide yourself in lies, and you don't have to guess what others want. Level with yourself, for you and you alone are responsible for your actions. Did you ever stop to think how much energy you have to use when you are lying? Living a lie takes a lot of joy from life.

Looking for Approval

Looking to others for approval and example can be a good experience only when you and those you look to are honest. This is powerful.

As you mature in life, you realize that you have to make a certain number of mistakes in order to achieve whatever goals you have set for yourself. So when you make a mistake, swallow hard and start over again. Don't be afraid to laugh at yourself. You see, we can be afraid to laugh at ourselves. We're afraid to make mistakes because we don't know how to start over again. We fear what others will think. You have to get on the bottom rung sometimes to be able to see where you are. You have to get down there to see things in perspective and see that it is not so impossible for you to go up. Once you feel yourself improving, you can be at ease just being you.

This is important. You aren't success or failure. You are you. No decision or act is as important as you. You are the one in control, and you are free to make decisions that will help you stay and feel OK.

We can measure ourselves by how we act during times of challenge and controversy. Are you afraid to disagree with your peers? Can you also be yourself when you know you are going along with the gang just to be part of things?

Think about how many waking hours you spent alone in the last seven days. Sometimes you can spend so much time getting into the mold of what others expect of you that you need some time alone to find yourself. Sometimes it is only through being alone that the world around you becomes a panorama to enjoy. If you have an opportunity to make a weekend retreat or a day of recollection, take it. We are born to seek and to find our place in life, and spending a good part of the time alone helps us to figure out just what it is we want and where that place is. How you use your time alone determines whether or not you'll succeed at learning to like yourself.

Life is a gift. How you use that gift, and how full your life can be depends on how you accept yourself and what you do with your energies and abilities. No one can use your energy or your abilities for you. Joy, sorrow, laughter, trials, all come in the package deal as you seek to find your way through life. Your experiences should never be left to fade out in your mind or be an ending in themselves. All your experiences should be ways to evaluate your progress, and they should constantly remind you that you are becoming more of yourself.

Checking You Out

Every now and then, try to take time out alone to think about the different moments in your life and ask yourself the following questions:

> When was I at peace with myself?
> What is hardest about me to live with?
> How can I live by the courage of my convictions?
> Am I a person of faith?
> Do I realize that I will not and need not escape my feelings?
> What feelings cause me the most trouble?
> What do I do about uncomfortable feelings?
> How can I look at my feelings and neither be trapped by them nor have to run away from them?

I recommend that you write these questions and tape them on the door of the john, on your bedroom door, or inside your locker. Every morning while you're starting your day, let this be a checklist. Let it sink in. Take the list with you when you sit in the tub (a perfect place for meditating). The three persons in you—me, myself, and I—can be great to be with and a source of strength for all who come in contact with you.

3. Why Am I Important?

Looking at Your Good Points

Did you ever wonder why you were born? Why you are here in this world right now? You know it's not accident. You are unique in the eyes of God, and you are also unrepeatable. There is no one else like you, nor can there ever be. So straighten your shoulders and keep your head high. You are you, and you are special. I know what you're thinking: Oh, she's gotta be crazy. Me, special?

I know you have weaknesses. I know it because we all have weaknesses. We are, after all, human. But we also have strengths. The main thing is to draw on our strengths, and then we can accept our weaknesses and see what we can do to correct them.

Don't dwell too long on your weaknesses. I want you to concentrate on your good points because you have so many good points that you don't even realize you have. Our strengths, our weaknesses, and our experiences all blend together to help us through our journey here on earth. You have an important mission to accomplish in life that is yours alone. Not anyone else's. Just yours. You have a special path to be walking, and only you can create that path and make it smooth. It's your unique path—your life. It's up to you to discover what your goals in life are and then to take steps to achieve those goals. Of course, discovering your goals is the hardest part. Imagine someone asking you what it is you want. It is not so simple to answer that question. It could take a good part of your lifetime to discover who you are, to solidify your values, and then to set your goals. But remember, there is a reason why you're here. It's up to you to make your stay here as meaningful as possible, to make your life as full as it can be.

Seeing You

How do you begin to do this? The first thing is to accept your individuality. Then you have to build on that individuality. This is important. Are you satisfied with your personality? If not, what are you going to do about it? Are you going to change to a better you?

Do you also like yourself? It is important to feel good about yourself in order to become more of yourself. Then people will begin to see, and to appreciate, the real you. You have to feel comfortable with who you are and what you represent to others before you can say, "I am special." I know it's hard to believe me when I tell you you're special, but when you yourself can say, "You know, I'm not so bad after all," that's the beginning of everything for you.

A few years ago there was a popular tune, "I've Gotta Be Me." It stressed the importance of being yourself. Frankly, when you think about it, there's nobody else you can be but yourself. This is the only way you can live with peace of mind. I really enjoyed listening to that song. It tells a lot about the singer, Sammy Davis, Jr., and about what he went through. How he struggled because of his race and because of what he was. He had to prove to people that no matter what color you are, no matter what kind of work you do, you're still the person God made.

Look around and think of some of your friends who try to "put on." Did you ever notice how unhappy they are trying to compete? What happens when there is constant competition? Sooner or later you are left alone with no one to share ideas with or pal around with. And what about people who do anything to be accepted? They're being used, and then eventually they're dropped. Is this the way you want to be accepted, and are these the people you want to live your life for? People who only know you when they need something?

When you work to be honest with yourself, you realize that you can't get something for nothing. But if you're honestly you, you won't need to compete or to be a "people pleaser."

Be True to You

Let your real self stand up and be counted. I also want you to realize that seeking and holding onto your identity is a lifetime job, not a one-shot deal. It involves constant reevaluation of yourself, your feelings, and your values, as well as constant holding onto what is precious to you—yourself.

I'm sure you've heard about famous people who have become hooked on expensive cars, sex, big-time spending, alcohol, drugs. What happened to them? They began to be appreciated for superficial things, and no one cared about who they were. The ego was never satisfied. Caught up in trivia, they began to think that their real selves were make-believe. When the glamour wore off, they realized that the real person was not there. And they couldn't live with that. They couldn't face themselves. Absorbed in the world of make-believe, when the real world came through, they began to crumble because of the emptiness that was revealed to them. But actually, all along, their real selves wanted to be noticed. It's hard to be true to yourself. Honesty costs us a lot of hard work. It doesn't just happen. Were these people true to themselves? Do they see their importance as people—or as actors?

Are you a person? Or are you an actor? Are you willing to face yourself, or are you role playing? Are you living in a world of make-believe—or are you living a real life?

Comparing Others to You

Do people compare you to your brothers or sisters? How do you feel about it? Do you like it when others wish that you were like Johnny? or Maria? "I never had to correct Johnny. He always knew what he was supposed to do. Maria was always neat and tidy." When parents or teachers compare you to a brother, a sister, or a classmate, don't you want to scream and say, "But I'm me! I'm not Johnny, Joey, Juanita, or Maria! I can't be like them. I'm just me!"

Adults don't always realize the impact of what they're doing even when you young people scream to be accepted as you are. Do you see what I'm getting at? Even you know you're unique. You know you're special. You know you're someone no one else can be. There is a line from Isaiah in the Bible ("I have called you by name") that really perks me up when I feel that people don't accept me for myself and only see me for the role I'm in—a lecturer, a speaker, a sister. People just take me for granted sometimes, and sometimes it gets me down. Isn't it great knowing that God calls you by name and not by a computer number. You are not one of the crowd, but you're Billy, Mary, Juan, Beth, Sotoko. How good it feels to be singled out by God.

Growing You

Look and see who you are today. I know you may not like all that you see. Growth depends on how well you accept what you are. What talents you have and where you're coming from. You have to face this realistically. We are all limited. You're not going to have what your friend has. You can't be who your friend is. But you have other talents, and they balance off. You might say, "Oh, I can't do this and I can't do that." But there is a lot worth doing that you can do if you want to.

Are you convinced you're a person of worth? I believe that you have a special contribution to make in this world we're living in. You and others make up this world. It becomes what you allow it to be. I mean that. Are you willing to take risks and encounter problems in a way that will be beneficial to others as well as to yourself? I think one of the first steps toward adulthood is the realization that whatever decisions you make somehow affect others. Once you understand this, you know that you have to think twice before you act.

Letting God Help

This is where God comes in. Do you trust God enough to do your best in a given situation, leaving the results in God's hands? At times we have to rely on God, even if we are in doubt. But it's up to you. God has created you to perform some definite service in the world. God has committed some work to you that he has not committed to another. You have your mission. You are a link in a chain, a bond of connection between persons. I found a piece written by John Henry Cardinal Newman, and I'd like you to look at it. Cardinal Newman really valued people. But most of all he valued himself, he saw how he fit

into the picture of the total society, and he saw his
responsibility to make it a better place. This is what
he said:

> God has created me to do him
> some definite service;
> he has committed some work to me
> which he has not committed to another.
> I have my mission . . .
> I am a link in a chain,
> a bond of connection between persons.
> He has not created me for naught.
> I shall do good. I shall do his work.
> I shall be an angel of peace,
> a preacher of truth in my own place
> while not intending it—
> if I do but keep his commandments.
> Therefore I will trust him.
> Whatever, wherever I am,
> I can never be thrown away.
> If I am in sickness,
> my sickness may serve him;
> in perplexity,
> my perplexity may serve him;
> if I am in sorrow,
> my sorrow may serve him.
> He does nothing in vain,
> he knows what he is about.

Stop for a moment and jot down the names of
people who are close to you in your family. Then

move out into a list of your friends, schoolmates, neighbors, and some of your cousins. You have created a chain. When you see how long this chain is, you begin to realize the importance of the connections between you and the people around you. I want you to repeat these words: *I have something to offer. I can do good. I can do God's work. I shall be a messenger of peace. A believer of truth in my own place while not intending it. If I do God's will I keep his commands.*

Your Closeness Chain

Fill in your name. Now name those of your family, friends, and others who are important to you and those to whom you are important.

I don't want you to walk down the street and say aloud, "God is good." I want you to act this out. People who see you act this out know that God is present. *"If I am in sickness, my sickness may serve him; in perplexity, my perplexity may serve him; if I am in sorrow, my sorrow may serve him."*

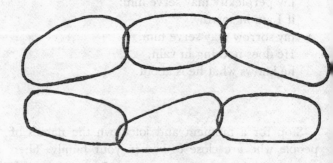

Being Comfortable with You

What I'm saying here is what I said before: be yourself by dealing with your feelings. Know what you feel, but turn those feelings over to God. If you're miserable that day, say, "Well, Lord, here I am, miserable. Accept me this way. I'm sorry this day. I had a death in the family (or my mother's sick, or whatever is wrong). This is me today. I am important. You gotta accept me. And if I'm happy today, accept the whole happy me and help me to use this day to be more me. Help me be more comfortable with myself, with others, and with you."

The influence you have on another person may make the difference in terms of how that person will respond to others and to God. How many times have you been influenced to action by friends or by a person you admired? Were they good experiences or ones you wish would fade out of the picture of your life? Each of us has the power to make or break another person. We have the power to give someone new hope or to kill that hope. The power to be yourself and to help others be themselves should make you think about a few things in your past. Remember, today you have a choice. Whatever you did in the past, today you can act according to what you believe. You don't have to fear or repeat the past.

How many times have you mocked or seen someone else mocking an older person walking down the street? You thought it was fun at the time. Did you ever stop to think that, whatever the other person's limitations, that person is important? How you treat others often says a lot about how you feel about yourself. We are all limited in some way, but we all receive unlimited love from God.

Have you ever decided to take a few candy bars or an apple from the grocery store? Did you know— or care—that the grocer has to pay for what was taken? Did you ever realize that if you don't pay, someone has to. You got away with it? Sure you'll get away with it. But did you really? At first, we all feel good about getting away with something. After all, few people are rewarded or noticed for doing good. But in the long run, what really makes you more you—more comfortable?

The influence you have on another person may cause the difference in terms of how that person will respond to others and to God. How many times have you been influenced to action by people or a person you admired. Were there times when you were influenced by someone you did not like or times you wish would fade out of the picture of

Looking Good

If I were to ask you to pause and jot down five bad points about yourself, you could do it in a few minutes. But if I were to ask you to jot down five good points about yourself, it would take longer. Why? Because you really don't think too highly of yourself. Jot down five good points about yourself.

—*Do you help people?*
—*Are you a good mathematician? Cook? Carpenter? Runner?*
—*Do you have a good personality? Some days?*
—*Are you always sad and grumpy?*
—*Do you pick on people?*
—*Do you enjoy life?*

My Five Good Points

1. _____

2. _____

3. _____

4. _____

5. _____

Try to jot down one good thing about two of your friends. It's often as hard to write something good about someone else as it is to write something good about yourself.

My Friends' Good Points

1. _____

2. _____

3. _____

4. _____

5. _____

We're so used to seeing the negative side of things and looking for weaknesses that we forget about the positive. Compliment a friend today. I want you to say something good about that person. Your compliment might be the beginning of a chain of compliments. That person you praised might feel so good that she or he will pass on a compliment to someone else, and so on throughout the world.

Having Talent

If you start looking at the positive side of yourself, you will begin to discover all the good points. Each day, try to come up with one good thing about yourself, and work on it. For example, you know you're good natured. Dwell on this thought today and share this happy side of yourself with your family and your schoolmates. If you're a good seamstress, help someone in sewing class today or at home. One of my sister's children is an excellent seamstress. I've always admired her skills in this area, but most of all I've admired her generosity in sharing her talent. She helps her schoolmates by sewing their prom gowns; she helps anyone else who asks for help. If I stop by at her house and ask if she has any spare time, she drops everything. She had a baby two weeks ago, and I went to see her. No matter how busy she was, she had time to help me out.

How many talents do you guys and gals have in mechanics or sports that you can share? That extra tip on how to grip the bat or hit a line drive, how to plan a meal, how to dress, how to arrange a trip, how to do a special wrist twist for the hook shot in basketball. If you take time each day to share some of the good in you, your talents or skills—or love—imagine what we who know you would have. Remember Jesus' message: don't hide your talents "under the bushel basket." There's nothing wrong with recognizing what you have and knowing it's good.

Believing in You

The films *Rocky* and *Rocky II* tell a story that we can all relate to. Rocky had this feeling of his own worth. Even though everyone thought he was a nobody, he knew he could be a winner; he knew he had what it takes to be on top. Why? Some force made him believe in himself. You have to believe in yourself in order for others to believe in you. Don't cut yourself short and cut yourself down. I know you have limitations. Who hasn't? You have to learn to live with your limitations and to make the most of them. Rocky encourages us to be realistic about ourselves. His story teaches us to accept our limitations and to share our talents. He makes us feel proud of our inner abilities. Do you feel noble? I know I'm noble. I feel noble. I'm proud of what I am; therefore I belong to nobility. Can you say you belong to nobility? Remember, Rocky started from scratch. I challenge you to do the same.

The spirit of life opens you to many surprises. Are you willing to embark on this lifelong adventure of developing your special self to the fullest? Life is a mystery that takes time to unfold, but your own vision of the world and of yourself in the world can make your life an exciting one. The decision remains with you as to how you will seize life's opportunities and surprises. No one can make these decisions for you. It is within your power to make your life an adventure or a dull and depressing situation that must merely be tolerated, as Thoreau said, in "quiet desperation."

Looking Closely

It is important to allow yourself a few minutes here and there to be alone with your thoughts. Riding on the bus to school, in the john in the morning while you're getting ready for school, while you're sitting in the tub, or in the evening before bed. Perhaps just sitting while you are waiting for supper to be ready. Break away for five minutes—that's all I ask—five minutes a day. Place yourself in a quiet mood and think about the events of the day. Because it is only during this stillness that you encounter God.

We are challenged to look at ourselves, to affirm our gifts and talents, to think of them as a way to serve our brothers and sisters, and to share all that we are given by giving our all to others. These ideas are powerful and enriching when I think of you, our future adults.

Nothing cripples personal potential more than the failure to see all that you have to offer. Granted, there are times when you're afraid to look inside yourself, but you have to. You have to face that special inner you.

The big cop-out in life is to blame our own failures on another person's words or attitudes. But let me tell you, no one can actually keep you from going toward your goal. No one can break you. It's up to you. That's the strength we have within us. That's why I say nothing cripples personal potential more than the failure to see what we have to offer. If you know what you have, then anyone can say anything to you and not hinder you. It is important that you and you alone feel a certain amount of pride and a sense of peace in whatever you have accomplished. If you have worked hard to achieve something, and if you have done so with honesty and integrity, then no one can take that away from you. You have the power to create your own happiness. You are charged with the task of developing your talents and your abilities, and this can come about only if you accept yourself. Your sense of self-worth has nothing to do with your size, shape, color, or achievement. It comes from within. You are created with a potential that allows your individual self to grow, to love, and to respond to others.

The psychologist Carl Rogers tells us, "I am more effective when I can listen to myself and can be myself." Can you listen to yourself? And be yourself? Are you part of what you're hearing? You see, you're special. Remember those words from Isaiah: "I have called you by name, you are mine." Don't disappoint those who have great faith in you.

4. Can I Be Different and Have Friends?

Being Different

Did you ever ask yourself these questions: Why am I so different? Why can't I be like someone else?

The reason you are so different is that you are a unique individual, fashioned only by God. There will never be anyone exactly like you. This thought should be a source of consolation and even joy to you—knowing you are special, original, unmatched. I bet at times you don't think that's true. For example, it can be traumatic when your science teacher springs a quickie quiz you were unprepared for and your classmates pass and you don't. You begin to wish you had more brains, like Juanita or Peter, so you could see how it feels to get good marks for a change. Did you ever stop to think that you might have other special skills? Are you a better athlete, musician, cook, or seamstress?

Think about what you have and not about wanting what somebody else has. If you become popular because you are a good listener—because you are your real self—this is great. You probably don't consider yourself Mr. or Miss Popular, but where it counts you are.

Somebody made me feel good one day. I had never realized I was good with teens, and I had been working with teens for eighteen years. I never would admit that I might be good at it because I thought that was pride—ego. I was reading somewhere about the qualities of a good youth worker. The article said that if you were comfortable being with the young, and if they were comfortable with you, then you really owed it to yourself to work with young people. This one sister was reading the same article and she said, "Hey, Sister Vinnie, this is you."

"Are you kidding, that's not me."

"Yeah, read it again," she said.

I felt guilty because I didn't want to admit that I was good at something, but once I admitted it, I felt comfortable with it. And it was a complimentary thing, it wasn't bad—imagine if it were a bad thing.

Here again is the idea of being honest with yourself. Some of you feel awkward and clumsy, and therefore you shy away from the crowd. In this stage of your life these feelings are all so normal. When your body is going through physical changes, you cannot always control what you do or the way you feel and act. You might say to me, "My friend doesn't act funny or talk weird, how come I do?" It will happen in time to your friend, too, or it may be happening and you just don't see it.

48

Feeling Different

You see, every one of us has our own special rate of growth. Some boys start to get a beard in seventh grade, some in tenth grade. So don't look down on others who are different from you.

Has your voice started to change? Do you feel you're walking funny? Or feeling strange or even sexy? Do you feel that other people think you talk funny and look weird?

This is a true story: I was talking to an eighth-grade girl (I'll call her Julie) last May, and she was kind of down in the dumps. She was very active in marathon running. She came in first in her county. But she didn't want to go out with her friends. Her friends were there to cheer her on, but they left her after the race. She used to leave the tournaments very sad instead of happy over her victories.

"Julie, what's wrong?" I asked her.

"The girls all think I'm a freak because I don't have my period yet. What's wrong with me?"

I began to tell her that she was OK. Some girls begin to menstruate in the fourth or fifth grade, and some don't until they are freshmen in high school. It was normal that she began her menstruating process a little later.

Feeling Pressured

It's unfair how we put pressures on ourselves and on one another for no reason at all. Why do we feel so bad if we are a little different? Take time to think about how others feel too. Remember, other people are also inexperienced and confused about themselves regarding their bodies and personalities.

You're at an age where you get acne, you have to wear braces on your teeth, and you begin to put on weight. These are signs that you are stepping out of childhood into adulthood. So don't mock your schoolmates now, for they have no control over their developing bodies. Start looking for personal assets you feel proud of, for example, your naturally beautiful wavy hair or your handsome physique. Our differences even out at the end, so look at yourself in a wholesome way without taking a negative slant.

If you need someone to talk to about the confusion you feel, don't be afraid to talk to the adults in your life. If you feel you can't talk to your teacher, there's always a school counselor or nurse who might be accessible. I think some teachers really care and want to be bothered. I know, if you admire somebody and they don't have time for you, that hurts. Don't be afraid to say, "I want to talk to you." Don't be afraid of hearing, "I don't have time." But usually, people will have time for you.

Being Tied Up

There is one thing that you and only you must do in order to be fully alive, and that is to accept yourself as you are. Not on the basis of what others say to you or about you. You have to be honest with yourself and just be. You can imprison yourself, as Rapunzel did, by listening to others. Rapunzel was a beautiful girl, but the witch convinced her that she was ugly and had her locked up in the tower. What kept her imprisoned was her fear: she didn't want anyone to see how ugly she was. Only when the prince noticed her and told her how beautiful she was, was she able to escape. Through the eyes of her prince, she realized she was pretty. He was her mirror.

Sometimes we need to look into the mirror of our friends' eyes or our parents' eyes to see how beautiful we are. Sometimes we are feeling lousy, but if someone says, "Gee, you look good," after a while we start feeling good. If you think you look horrible and don't like the way you dressed today, you feel uncomfortable because you don't want to be walking around. If you think you look great, you feel great. I'm trying to help you have more to say about how you feel and act.

How many of you are familiar with the song "Georgy Girl"? It's about a carefree girl who goes up and down the avenue window-shopping, running here and there, breezing through, seeming so happy-go-lucky. She wears a mask. She doesn't want to be known. It's not her real self that she projects. The real Georgy is a lonely person, but she runs away from her feelings of need. She doesn't want people to see how alone and scared she is. She puts on.

Being Special

How many times have you worn a mask hiding something? Have you ever tried to hide the fact that you are Italian, Puerto Rican, or Polish, so you wouldn't be mocked by your friends? There was a time in the history of America when people felt they should assimilate—that they should lose the unique characteristics of the country they came from. In recent years, people have wanted to identify once more with their origins and have begun to take pride in their particular heritage. We now know that hiding your individual cultural identity can be dangerous, for in doing this you are blocking out an important part of your inheritance—your nationality. Until you face the fact that you do belong to a certain group, and until you learn to be proud of it, you will be an unhappy person. You might be subject to ethnic jokes, but the way you handle these jokes and learn to laugh with them and at them helps you to know who you are and what you stand for. If you can be unashamed of who you are, jokes will not be detrimental to you.

When people tell me Italian jokes, I laugh with them, and they feel comfortable. How you accept such humor may be a reflection of how you accept yourself. In instances like this, you have to make a judgment on each individual situation. I know a person who hates Italians, so when she tells an ethnic joke, I know what she means, and I don't laugh. I know another person who's a nut and tells jokes on all ethnic things. When she tells me an Italian joke,

I crack up. She's a wonderful nut. She doesn't use it as a dig. It's fun.

Standing Alone

Each of us has a Georgy girl inside dreaming of being someone other than who we really are. Last week I was talking with a fourteen-year-old boy in Connecticut. He was upset about having to go to a rock concert. He didn't want to go. He didn't care about this group or the music they produced. He would rather go to see another group or to a different concert if he could. His friends were pressuring him to go, but deep down he didn't want to, yet he couldn't tell them. "I don't want to be different and not go," he told me. "My friends will drop me."

The boy was mistaken. You have to remember that you are an individual equipped to make your own decisions. You don't need your friends or your gang to make decisions for you. I told him that I wished he had guts enough to be his own person.

He called me a couple of days ago to tell me that, despite the consequences, he decided not to go. The gang went without him, and to his surprise they bought him a T-shirt as a souvenir.

I hope you gained a little courage in reading this. Perhaps it made you examine how you feel and think in certain matters. You don't have to go along with hairstyles and clothes or wear a comb in your back pocket because everyone else is doing it. Try starting your own fad that you feel comfortable with. Try being different. If your gang would drop you for being a little different, do you want to belong to that gang?

Have you ever been called a string bean because you're skinny, a giraffe because you're tall, or fat because you're overweight? How do you handle it? You know people are often teased about some part of their anatomy—a fat stomach, skinny legs, acne, a high voice when other boys have low ones. Did it ever occur to you that people may tease out of fear that they don't want to be like the person they are teasing? It's up to you and the way you react whether or not the teasing will continue. Don't be open for it. Don't ask if anyone thinks you are pretty or how muscular you look. Don't let on that teasing bothers you. In time, the gang will stop.

Belonging to a gang can make one act tough and nasty toward outsiders. We don't want this. Is it right? Are you hurting someone's feelings just to stay in the group? This is unjust and pretty low. Another way of dealing with teasing is to turn a negative into a positive. For example, Mel Tillis, the famous country singer, is a stutterer, but when he sings he doesn't stutter. When people joke about him he goes along with it because he knows he can't do anything about it. But he does know he has a talent, and he draws on his talent, which I think is wonderful. Other examples are playing an instrument or dancing. I'm sure with the new disco craze you can come up with some exciting steps to teach others. Draw on something other than what you are teased about, and I guarantee you'll get a far different response. Little by little you'll find yourself accepted by the group because you rose above the teasing by being yourself. You didn't go along with the game.

Being a Friend

We can be different from each other and still be good friends. Is your relationship with a friend that of friendship or of slavery? Do you go along with everything he or she says or does? Do you realize that at times you have to, and can, say no to certain demands made by your friends? You don't have to agree on everything all the time regarding your social life, the way you dress, and things that you do. You have to leave space in your friendship to allow for differences in personality and opinions. You can love somebody, but you don't have to go along with everything they say. And that won't take anything away from the love, either.

Let me explain what I just bombarded you with. There were six teen-age boys who were staying together. One of them decided that the gang should go to a movie on a school day. Everyone thought it was a great idea. Then the boy told the others that during the movie they were going to sit in the balcony and throw popcorn down on other people and also that this was a good chance to get a few puffs on their cigarettes. One of the boys came to me after it was over. He was upset, but not because they got thrown out of the theater. He was mad at himself for not standing on his own two feet and not saying no to the whole thing. The reason he came to me was because he made one of my retreats. He was right. He should have stood on his own feet, but he didn't. And that's why he was angry with himself. He was so afraid that someone in the theater would get hurt that he didn't have such a good time after all. His parents grounded him for two weeks, but what bothered him most was that he wasn't man enough to say no.

Friendship encompasses so much that it can make demands that sometimes tear us apart. You can have friends, but you don't have to go along with things that bother you just because you want to belong. In the end, when it all blows over, your friends, if they're true ones, will come back to you.

If your friends smoke pot, do you have to? Here is another test of your character. Do you like your friends well enough to say, "Come on, we really don't need that stuff"? Just because others are doing it doesn't mean you have to. What I'm saying here is, do you have the courage to say no?

Reasons You Are My Friend

List the names of two of your friends in the space below. After naming your friends, list four reasons why you like each. Are they generous, fun-loving, helpful? I'm sure you can come up with a lot of good answers.

My friend, _____
I like my friend because:

1. _____

2. _____

3. _____

4. _____

My friend, _____
I like my friend because:

1. _____

2. _____

3. _____

4. _____

Begin to dwell on these good points, and in a subtle way, remind your friends of them. For example, you might say, "Remember when we used to ride our bikes in the park? Gee, I really miss those times." Try to sway your friends from doing something that may spell trouble. I ask you again, is your friendship wholesome or that of enslavement?

Nowadays, one big thing among kids is to see how much beer you can drink before you get drunk. What bothers me most is that you do it just to prove you're big, without realizing the harm you're doing to yourself. During the eighth-grade retreat day I was conducting, a girl mentioned to me that her best friend made her promise not to tell her parents that she was drinking heavily. The girl came to me because she was worried about her friend. She was concerned about how to help. She was torn between her loyalty as a friend and seeking outside help.

It's hard when you have a friend you want to help and that friend does not allow you to help. I think there are times when you have to decide to take the initiative. Sometimes you have to put your foot down and say, "Yeah, I am your friend, and this is why I am doing what I'm doing." This was a major decision, and I admire the girl for making it. It is not easy to do what you think is the right thing. She wouldn't drink with her friend. She constantly begged her to lay off the booze. Her friend said, "If you are my friend, you'll go along with me."

I told that girl that in seeking help she was acting as a true friend. Later on, I spoke to the girl who had the problem. At first she was angry and felt betrayed, but after a while she realized that her friend saved her from ruining herself. Have you ever been confronted with a similar problem? It is a heart-breaking experience. How do you feel toward your friend?

Sharing and Caring

One of the ingredients involved in a good friend-ship is respect for the other person, even though he or she is different in many ways. It is important that we respect and uphold the values of a friend's life—his or her like or dislike of certain foods, clothing, or forms of entertainment. Another important in-gredient in a relationship is acceptance of differ-ences. We have to realize that we are individuals made up in a unique way by a loving God. There-fore, we have certain habits, likes, and dislikes. This makes life exciting and interesting. I am delighted when my friend shows me that she thinks and feels things differently from the way I do. I love to listen to her explanations of why she likes this movie or that dress. No matter how long you know someone, there's always a little mystery to be revealed. There are intriguing and fascinating factors involved in a wholesome relationship.

Another important ingredient, and a hard one at that, involved in building friendships is bending. Are you willing to bend a little? To not seek your own way all the time and to go along with what your friend prefers to do for a change? Provided it isn't harmful. This can involve a lot of giving on your part and on your friend's part also. For friendship has to go two ways. There has to be a give-and-take on both parts. This takes in the whole aspect of respect. What each person means to the other. Not holding back, but a complete moving forward to a strong bond of friendship that sometimes lasts a lifetime.

Disagreeing

We forget that relationships consist at times of conflicts and disagreements. Did you ever have an argument with your friend over something and perhaps you were unwilling to unbend a little? How did you feel the next time you met up with your friend? Did you put your head down, turn your eyes away? Did you feel guilty or angry? It might be hard to imagine at first, but it is possible to learn how to sit and talk about something that you disagree on. It is very hard when we start to confront people—even when we do it in a nice way, without bad feelings. Did you feel uneasy? Even more than uneasy, did you feel your mouth quiver, as if you might cry? Did you have a hard time knowing how to begin or find it difficult getting the words out? These are normal reactions, but the way you handle them depends on how much this friend means to you. There's a song called "We Just Disagree" by Dave Mason. There's a line in it that talks about leaving things alone when people can't see eye to eye. You can hold onto a grudge, or you can drop the whole thing and begin again where you left off, which I think would be healthier if you can't bend or you can't see eye to eye. In any relationship you remain an individual; therefore, you are what you are, and what you think is your own. Sometimes how you feel and think cannot be changed, but you can accept the differences of opinion of your friend or friends. You have to remember that you have your own values, ideas, and goals; they identify what kind of person you are. Relationships give us opportunities to share ourselves with others even if we don't always agree. At these times, we don't take each other for granted, and we can learn to respect a difference in viewpoint. Times like these require openness, respect, and forgiveness from both parties. We find it so hard to say, I'm wrong, I'm sorry, yet that's the most beautiful thing to say—"I'm sorry. I'm going to change." In the Gospels, Jesus challenges us with these three elements: admitting error, being sorry, and being willing to change. Since conflicts are always going to be with us, perhaps we can better approach them in a Christian way.

5. Do I Have to Go Along with the Gang?

Being at Ease

Have you ever found yourself in the following position: One day your teacher announced that she thought it would be good for the whole class to do a community project. The teacher came up with the idea of repainting the community center so that the senior citizens could have a place to go to during the day. You really got excited about the project, but when your teacher asked for volunteers, you were afraid to raise your hand. You weren't sure what the gang would think of you. You were scared, and you were relieved when the teacher backed off, even though you were hoping to be called on so you wouldn't look like a volunteer.

Don't feel bad if this sort of thing has happened to you. It is perfectly natural. What counts is how you overcome this fear of what the gang will say. You will like yourself better if you have the courage to be an individual. Don't be chained by your friends' opinions. For you have to make your own decisions and show others that you have a mind of your own. Why should you be intimidated and therefore held back from something you really want to do?

One day I said, "Look at how dirty this classroom is. What a mess. I don't know what I'm going to do about it."

"Gee, I like to paint, sister," said one of my students. "Let me give it a good paint job."

Before you know it, the whole class started volunteering because one person said, "Yeah, I like that idea."

For just a moment, I want you to reflect on your gang. Figure out how many times they supported you and how many times they tore you down because of what you did. Hopefully, the first column will outweigh the second. But nine out of ten times it doesn't. The support is not there. Gangs have no conscience, even though individual members do.

It makes you feel good to belong to a gang, but you are taking a chance when you're accepted by them. Do you need to be pressured? Don't you want to run your own life? In belonging to a group, we can become afraid to do what makes us happy. Sometimes we get so caught up in what the gang expects of us that we forget we are individuals with our own ideas, feelings, and choices.

Being in a Gang

Following are some examples of how the gang can influence you:

(1) One person who has a little bit of push in the

gang doesn't have the assignment ready, so word is passed around that nobody should hand in the assignment today.

(2) Even if you don't drink, the gang says you have to keep quiet about those people in the gang who drink—or use dope—even if you're asked.

In other words, you have to do anything they say just to stay within the group. In your desire to belong, you might forget that you have feelings and that you have a choice to make here. Your feelings, your choices, your values, that all gets pushed aside. The gang takes precedence. You lose your individuality. You lose your identity.

I want you to think of a time when you wanted to do something but were afraid because the gang wouldn't like it. How did you feel? I bet you felt rotten and maybe pretty low in your opinion of yourself. Was it worth it? How did you feel toward your friends? Did you like them? Were you angry with them as well as with yourself?

It isn't easy to belong to a gang. But it's important that you have friends. And what we're dealing with is how you learn to be yourself while being part of a group. Peer pressure is important if it's used right. Belonging to a group is important. But you have to learn how to deal with a group and be your own self as well.

Being Pushed

How many of you are familiar with the television series "The White Shadow"? In this you can see a lot of what I'm talking about. It deals with the pressures, as well as the benefits, of belonging to a gang. The next time you view this program or another like it, imagine yourself as one of the characters and see how you would react.

In the book *Sticks and Bones* by Lynn Hall, a young man becomes friends with a gay person. The gang discovers this friendship and accuses the young man of being gay. They treat him badly. This unjust judgment and cruel treatment affected the young man for the rest of his life, yet he did not deny his friendship.

Are you being controlled by your gang? If the gang decided that the whole group was going to skip school on Friday, would you? That's peer pressure. This is the time when you should take a good close look at yourself and examine your values. How do you feel about yourself? And how do you value those around you? The thing that should be uppermost in your mind is that you are a unique individual with ideas of your own and a mind of your own. That's how you exercise your individuality and that shows what kind of a person you are. You must develop a self and you must respect yourself. Only then will others do the same. Don't let your friends take this important element away from you. You don't have to go along with things you don't agree with.

Drinking

A problem that we really must talk about in this chapter is drinking. Why do you get drunk? If you're doing this for status, I ask you, is it worth it? Do you want to be labeled an alcoholic at the age of fourteen just to be in with the crowd? It's not worth it, especially when you have a life ahead of you.

If a young person is truly an alcoholic, and he or she starts drinking at this age, you must believe that alcoholism is a disease. A fourteen-year-old girl came to me with a drinking problem. She was all mixed up. Actually, she felt she had nothing to live for. I reacted, plenty. She got involved in drinking because her girl friends told her it was the thing to do to be popular. Everything was great for a time, but all of a sudden her friends dropped her and her classmates looked down on her and began to label her "alky." Is this what you want?

If you should drink and discover that you have a problem with it, then you don't have a choice. That girl had no choice about being an alcoholic, and she only discovered it when she began to drink. She also found out that her friends weren't able to understand her, especially if they weren't alcoholics, and that they would only look at her as something low or bad. They didn't want her around anymore, so now she had two problems. One was having a disease called alcoholism; the other was having her friends misunderstand her. This is a good example of one of the problems of peer pressure. You drink because the group approves of it, but then you find out that, unlike other people, you can't stop and you want to get drunk and have to. Do you have classmates who have alcohol in their lockers? Who go home at noon to have a drink or more and (even though they are supposedly intelligent or popular) hang around with people who get into trouble because of drinking?

You have a choice. You don't have to pick up a drink. That's the first thing you should be aware of. You don't have to pick up a drink. If anyone taunts you or accuses you of being afraid that you're an alcoholic and can't drink, it's all right, particularly if you have good reasons to be afraid. You may have a father or mother or brother or sister or aunt or uncle who is an alcoholic. The best place to try alcohol is not with a group of young people. How about discussing it at home? If you've done it already you don't have to continue doing it, but if you find you can't stop on your own then you may have this disease that a lot of people in our society have. You didn't choose to have the disease any more than you would choose to have diabetes, Addison's disease, any of those things.

But you can choose to accept the fact that you have the disease and then turn around and do something about living. There are opportunities for young people with alcohol problems today. There's Alateen, which is a division of Alcoholics Anonymous, and there's young people's A.A. The church thinks the problem is so important that a whole group of priests, sisters, and lay people have formed a group called the National Clergy Council on Alcoholism.

Alcoholism is not a moral disease, but drinking can be a serious problem. That's all. To drink and to do things that are irrational or are going to get you in trouble may not mean that you're an alcoholic, but still, you are in trouble because you're doing something you can't handle. And the excuses that adults do it too, or that your buddies have done it, are not valid. Thousands of adults go to jail every year because of things they do while drinking. There are murders and robberies; there are automobile accidents where drunk drivers kill innocent people. Alcohol in itself is not bad, any more than sugar is bad. How you use it, or whether or not you use it, is what's important. If a diabetic eats sugar, that diabetic gets sick. If an alcoholic drinks alcohol, that alcoholic gets sick.

Choosing Action

Think seriously about what you should do and shouldn't do when you are with the gang.

Remember, you are a loser or a winner depending on what path you choose. I hope you can see by the gradual change that takes place regarding a person's conduct and personality as the person progresses in drinking. This can be avoided. There is an ancient Hebrew legend that tells the difference between moderate and heavy drinking:

> When Noah planted grapevines, Satan revealed to him the possible effects of alcohol.

He slaughtered a lamb, a lion, an ape, and a pig. He explained: "The first cup of wine will make you mild like a lamb; the second will make you feel brave like a lion; the third will make you act like an ape; and the fourth will make you wallow in the mud like a pig."

A researcher on hallucinations made this statement regarding LSD: "LSD is an invitation to temporary insanity for all, and possibly permanent insanity for some." One of my former students is institutionalized today because of LSD and other drugs. He tried everything that was on the market until the drugs ate out his brain, cell by cell. Today he is a human vegetable. Why? Simply to be with the gang.

Being You

I would like to share a reflection written by one of my former students who was dealing at the time with pressure from her friends to be part of the group. She wanted to belong.

A Color Wheel

It's just like every different color on it is like
the personalities of people.
Some are good and some are bad, but we're all
equal, but how?
The wheel turns from red to blue to green . . .
we change from good to bad or bad to good,
we'll never know . . .
We're all different, but then again all the same
in our ways.
As all the colors meet, they change. When we
meet different people, we change or they do.
The color wheel is like a person who is all
mixed up . . . they don't know what to do.
Should I have this friend or not?
The color wheel got made by experimenting;
so we should just try, maybe it will work out,
maybe it won't, you just gotta wait and see . . .
A color wheel is different, every color is different. People are different—good, bad, black,
white, fat, skinny—yet we're all the same.
We just have to act like ourselves. Don't try to
be a big shot if you're not.
Be what you are, not what people make you—
just like a color wheel is the way it is.

You can see what she's dealing with. We're all different, but then again we're all the same. She uses images that a person who was all mixed up would use. This is how she was. She didn't know what to do. Should she have this friend or not? Life, like the color wheel, is often lived by experiment. Try. Maybe what you want will work out; maybe it won't. You have to try, and see. This girl's home situation had been very confused since her father moved out. She was running away from it.

You just have to be what you are, not what people make you. The color wheel is a powerful image. To be part of a group can require a lot of courage. It takes guts to know when to go along with the gang and when not to. Truthfully, when you do something wrong and get caught, you have yourself to blame, not the gang. You are the one who decided whether you wanted to go along with them. If the gang you belong to can't let you feel good about you, then it is up to you to decide whether or not you want to remain with them. If you choose to stay with them, that choice is freely made, and you have yourself to answer to.

6. Does Anyone Know How I Feel?

Knowing Your Feelings

Sometimes it may be hard to believe, but your years as a teen-ager can be some of the best times of your life. I hope you will be able to look back on these years and agree with this statement. Your friends during these years will have a great influence on your life. Can you look back proudly on them? I hope you will be able to say that they helped you become what you are today.

When I ask young people what they want, what comes out loud and clear is the question, Does anybody know how we feel? You want to know if others care how you feel. You seem to want an opportunity to express your feelings.

You are in a period of your life when you begin to experience uncertainty, self-doubt, and suffering. You wish others would listen for a change instead of coming out with rash statements. During this painful period, it is beneficial to be able to express how you feel. You need someone to bounce ideas off on how you feel about yourself and the everyday events in nitty-gritty life.

Understanding

Did you ever find yourself wanting to scream out, "Stop—listen—you have it all wrong. This is not the way I feel!" Many young people feel this way with their parents or in school. Sometimes you feel condemned before you're judged. We adults at times tend to label things and people without investigating the situation and what is entailed. We make our judgment, and that's that. I wish to apologize if we have caused you pain because of this attitude. How many times have you experienced something like this? You are given a homework assignment, and when you go home after school you find that your mother isn't feeling well and has gone to bed. You are stuck with cooking, cleaning, dishes, or taking care of your little sister or brother. In the meantime, you keep thinking about this science project you're supposed to be doing. When you discuss the situation with your parents, they tell you not to worry, your teacher will understand.

But when you go to school and present the problem to your teacher, she gives you an untrusting look. She says she's heard that story before, and she tells you to stay after school every day until you finish the assignment. You're crushed, and you feel misunderstood. And rightly so.

I've seen instances where young people are helpless. Then the grown-ups want to know why they lose respect. I'm so sorry to say that I have talked to many teens who have experienced this. What do you do? Really, what counts here is how you feel about yourself. You alone have to live with yourself. You could have run away from the situation, but you chose to help your mother.

Doing Good

One thing missing in my formal education was an important lesson. And that is that everything I do because I believe it is right may not be accepted, rewarded, or even understood by others. I always thought that when you did good, you would be rewarded. The truth of the matter is, you aren't. Sometimes people misunderstand your intentions. Sometimes you get punished for doing something you believe is right. You can't do only what others want you to do or only what others approve of. You have to do something because you think it's good. Otherwise, when you get no reward, no approval, or no understanding, you're going to feel cheated. The only good reason for doing the right thing is that you think it's the right thing. It took me a long time to come to that conclusion. I used to get so disappointed. I wondered why, when I did all those things, people didn't recognize what good I was trying to do. The reason for being a Christian is not to obtain a reward or to make you feel that you are among the majority of the people. When you presume that the majority of people always do good and use that as a reason for your behavior, you're going to be disappointed. The majority of people may be trying to lead good lives, but we can't presume that they're going to do so every day, or that they will be understood by everyone every day. It doesn't work that way. And the reason I'm putting it in the discussion here is because I think it's important for me to share it with you. You're no different from me. No one is going to constantly pat either one of us on the back for doing good. Even if others always did understand, approve, or reward us for what we said or did, the only way to really feel good within ourselves and in healthy relationships is to understand that there is a power greater than us, or the gang, or our parents, or anybody. Call that power God, call it Jesus, call it the Holy Spirit; call it whatever. If you have a relationship with that power, you also know that you're in tune with something greater than you. This is where you get a chance for peace within yourself. This is the only way to know yourself. You have to live with each decision you make.

And you know, no matter what you say to that teacher or anybody else in a similar situation, you're starting to make it. You can't change that teacher's mind either. So you must swallow hard sometimes and say to yourself, well, I know I can live with myself.

Doing First Things

So stop trying to go back to change somebody else's mind. You can't. Their minds may change in

76

time when they get to know you better (and sometimes they don't).

I can remember incidents that seemed so important to me that I thought, people must think I'm awful. And now those same people say to me, "Oh, that was just something that happened, but that isn't who you are." That's wild. Of course you have to be in your thirties to ever hear things like that.

I think it's good to express how you feel at the moment; don't wait. And don't wait till a person's dead to tell them how great they are. It's great to hear good stuff when you're alive and you can enjoy that compliment because you don't get compliments that often.

You've presented an explanation for your behavior. It was rejected. It then becomes the other person's problem. You have done all you can. When things cool down and the opportunity arises again, try again. I've found that in time the truth all comes out. Then you have some adults that have to do a lot of apologizing. If they're mature enough to do it. Some don't even bother. That's the crushing experience. If you are right, then the waiting period shouldn't be too hard because you have been justified within yourself, and this is all that matters. You are who you are in your own self, and it is important to be able to live with yourself with a clear conscience. It sounds so easy but it isn't. It's very hard to swallow.

Listening to a Conscience

You have to start developing a clear conscience. It entails the whole idea of being comfortable with yourself. You know how you feel when you have done something wrong and you don't own up to it. It seems to me that conscience is not a little voice back there saying, "Watch it, you're doing the wrong thing." Conscience seems to be listening to your inner self, hearing a spirit, a will, or a power greater than yourself. The development of a conscience seems to provide you with the opportunity to take the time to listen to yourself and to make the distinction between acting out of fear and acting out of faith. We often do things because we're afraid we're going to get punished or caught at doing wrong. Some people are challenged by the idea of seeing if they can avoid getting caught. I see a conscience as being a tool to help me be me. My conscience helps me take the time to ask what it is I really think I want to do in a given situation. It helps me to decide what I can do that will be good for me in the long run, not just in the short run.

In the Long Run

For example, if I steal that candy bar, I'm going to feel good right now (if I get away with it) because I want the candy bar. But when I think about the long run, I realize that I could go to jail. First of all,

I don't want to go to jail, and second, I'm causing someone else a problem. If I steal because I want to see if I can get away with it, that's bad for me because it builds a self-destructive attitude. Every time I get away with it, I keep being challenged to go for something more. With that attitude, eventually it's hard to know the difference between what is right and what is wrong. So the real danger is not in going to jail. The danger is that I might confuse my sense of the difference between right and wrong. I might forget to take the time to ask what is the right thing for me to do in the long run. I think part of the confusion young people and adults have is remembering what is *best in the long run*. When we choose to act, we must remember that the consequences of our actions involve more than reward or punishment. Everything we do has an effect that we can't measure. No action of ours stops with us. We can choose to live a full life, or we can choose to live a narrow life of self-centeredness.

It's important to have a friend your age to talk to. It's important to belong to a group that accepts you, for you need to feel "at ease" enough to be able to express how and what you feel. Everyone needs to talk on a gut level. Sometimes it is hard to express your feelings when you feel different from others. You should try to get yourself to be free enough to express yourself and not be afraid of what others might say. You can't live your life in fear that others will talk down to you or yell at you because you expressed how you felt. This is why there are so many different sports, clubs, societies—in school and in life in general—so that everyone can find or make a space to feel at ease.

Expressing Yourself

Each person has a voice and a need for expression. Yet a group can become the place where you lose your individuality and your ability to be different in expressing yourself. Peer pressure and extreme concern over what others think about what you do, say, or believe can be so destructive that they keep you from being you.

You are at an age when you think about people of the opposite sex. You're finding out about your body. Your body has new rhythms, and you have to learn to feel comfortable with these rhythms. At times feelings come over you that you are unable to express. If you are afraid or ashamed, try to talk about your feelings with your father or mother or a friend who is much older than you. Choose someone you feel comfortable with to talk about your romantic feelings regarding a boy or a girl. I know a lot of my friends' children talk to me because they have a hard time talking to their parents. Talking to some adult you trust would be a healthy step on your part toward arriving at a mature sense of balance in dealing with your feelings.

You see, we all have mixed-up feelings, but many of us don't feel free to express them for fear of being rejected.

Adults too find it hard to express how they feel. This is why at times you should take the lead with your parents. Ask them why they say certain things to you. For example, your mother may tell you that she doesn't want you to hang around with a certain group of girls. She leaves it at that, with no explanation. Instead of growing resentful and angry, wait until a more convenient time and ask her why. This happened to me when I was an eighth grader. I was hanging around with a fast group of girls who talked only about their figures, dating, and doing what they pleased.

The girls and their conversation really enticed me.

Ask Why

After a month of this, my mother came out openly and frankly, saying, "I don't want you to stay in that group. Your other friends give you more of a chance to be you." I got furious and stormed out of the house. The next day at breakfast mother and I were alone. I asked her why she objected to these girls. To me they were really great. She told me she had heard that they were experimenting with sex and with smoking. She said she didn't want me to get hardened like them. I wasn't cross with what she told me, but the next time I went with the girls I listened more carefully to what they said, and I realized how true it all was. I often wondered where I would be today if I hadn't stopped and asked why. Some kids get resentful, and instead of asking why they'll stay with a gang out of spite.

Growing Up

There's an excellent book by Joyce Maynard called *Looking Back*. The author was eighteen when she wrote it. She tells how she felt about growing up, and she talks about the things she did to be accepted in the gang. All through the book you can feel along with her. She is expressing feelings that she was afraid to express when she was growing up.

She shares my thoughts with you. Here is an excerpt about how she felt when she went to school dances.

> More important to me than the computer issue, though, in 1967, was the whole question of going to the dance. It seems odd to me now, reading in that diary, of my reluctance to ask my parents whether I could go. They would have said yes, of course, and they would have been surprised that I even bothered to ask. But (and this is where my fear came in) they would also have been surprised that I wanted to go— that I, who worked so hard at being grown up and cool and analytical, would want to put myself in the sweaty hands of some skinny, slicked-down, Old Spice-y thirteen-year-old. Because in my head, I wasn't a day under

thirty-five. So when my mother asked me, "What boys do you like best?" I laughed and said they were all terrible (and so young) and was amazed at the openness with which some of my friends exposed their crushes. Relishing them and never, like me, ashamed.

I was ashamed of my wanting to go to the dance and of my hidden store of purple eye-shadow and inky eyeliner that I revealed the moment I emerged, after hours in the bath-room, as from a beating, with bruised-looking, shakily outlined eyes and lips so whitened with Yardley slicker that I appeared almost mouthless.

I went alone to dances, I'd come right home from school and that day would wash and set my hair and put my dress on, hours early, tak-ing Seventeen-model poses before the mirror, dancing in silence with the door closed, run-ning downtown for last-minute purchases of earrings or nail polish, curling my eyelashes, as if that was all I needed—curlier lashes—to get a partner so that next time I wouldn't have to go alone. My father always offered to drive to the dance (so did my mother—she would pull up slowly to get a look at all the boys and point out the cute ones, while I sank in the seat and hoped she wouldn't kiss me good-by). Most often, though, I walked, with a scarf around my head to keep my hair from blowing and two quarters in my pocket for admission.

Can you find yourself in this situation? We do many things during our lives. We believe many things and speak out when necessary to uphold our values. As we mature, we begin to set goals for ourselves. We also begin to develop attitudes pertaining to our feelings about things, our interests, and our friends. During these times, our emotions are displayed in various forms. How we master them shows what kind of character we have. Do you ever find yourself lonely because there is no one who will listen to how you feel? You feel so alone and frustrated when you try to communicate your feelings and thoughts and no one is hearing a word? I find young people constantly saying to adults, "You're not hearing; you're not listening. I'm talking, but you don't know what I'm talking about." And you get so frustrated that you get to the point where you don't care. We get frustrated when no one understands our viewpoints on certain issues. During debates in class, do you ever get frustrated when your ideas aren't accepted or listened to? We can get so absorbed in our frustrations that we get emotionally drained. Often we need to do something for ourselves—to get away from it all, for example, going on a camping trip for the weekend; going to a ball game, a movie, or a retreat; or taking up a hobby. We need a sense of balance in life. But don't just do what your friend is doing. Although it may be an outlet for your friend, it may not be one for you. It may be a way of communicating for your friend, but not for you. You need your own unique way of amusing yourself and of expressing yourself; you need to release your frustrations in your own way. Don't do only what your friend does.

A good image here is dancing shoes. Each dancer's shoes fit her or his feet. Each kind of dancing requires a special shoe. Maybe today you'll wear tap-dance shoes. Tomorrow your friend will be wearing ballet shoes while you wear disco shoes. The type of "dancing" shoes that will fulfill our needs can be unique for each person who puts them on.

Looking Closely

As we grow older, we realize that we need space and time away from everyday pressures. To attain a necessary sense of balance, we must examine our interests and our needs, as well as our dreams. We shouldn't let one aspect of life take up all our time. Too often we tend to dwell on one thing, especially because our world right now seems very small and what we are doing seems very important. Often our vision is centered on ourselves, so one issue can be magnified out of perspective for months. The idea of trying to get into your dancing shoes means trying to get a clear head and a clear vision. Life is most comfortable and fulfilling when we don't let one aspect of life take up all of our time. Life is not meant to entrap us. What we should do is discover which set of extra shoes or life roles we want to accept in order to be ourselves.

7. I Am for Others

Being Accepted

Have you ever asked yourself what you mean to others? What is your place in the world? Where you belong? With whom you belong? How you affect the lives of your parents, brothers, sisters, and friends?

We so want to be accepted by our families. We can say how great we are, but somehow something seems missing unless we can go to our family for support. I think I could be given all the honors in the world, but if my religious community—my family—is not saying "We're supporting you, we're behind you," that honor would mean nothing to me. Deep down, young people want their parents' support more than anything else. Our friends are a temporary support to keep us going. Don't worry if things aren't perfect at home today; we often don't develop full relationships with our parents until we go away to school, get a job, or get married, and then come back knowing who we are.

Reaching Out

We put together a high school program. We had about three hundred young people in the program, and it was on the Old and New Testament. I formed a council because I didn't know most of the young people. We did one project a month. One Old Testament project was on Joseph and his brothers. I told students I could get a movie about the story, and one of them said, "Let's call the project 'A Night Out with Joe and His Friends.' "

I said, "Good, let's have 'A Night Out with Joe.' "

Another said, "Can we invite our parents?"

"Sure."

I told the teachers to save all the projects, all the homework, all the work done, and we would have an open house.

We made invitations and sent them to the parents. Young people wanted their parents to know they weren't fooling around at night. Every Monday night they came to this program. They wanted their parents to know this. They were proud to show what they had done. That meant more to them than anything else. Yet they would never say it. This evening was their way of expressing it.

The students made popcorn. They served drinks. They showed the movie. When the parents came, it was unbelievable. The young people had decorated the hall. As you walked down into the basement, which is the school hall, you entered the city of Jerusalem. There were palm trees, made out of the posts. They had the tavern, and they had bread they called manna, and they had all the projects they had done and all their work. It was fantastic.

Every once in a while you get a warm feeling inside because you feel you were helpful to someone or said something that made someone happy. Maybe you said, "Gee, mom, you look tired today, I'll come home and do the wash." Boy, it brightened her day. Young people do that sometimes. Sometimes you can be tremendous. I don't ask much of you. All I do expect of you is to be yourself so that you can share the qualities you have with everyone you touch during the day. If I am genuinely concerned for others, then I am going out and seizing the opportunities and working to change at least the portion of the world I live in. Are you ready and willing to take the risk to change things around you to make this a better world? Think about it. You can be classified as a loafer or a worker. The loafer is one who watches TV day in and day out, sitting in front of a snack tray. A loafer is a person with no interest, no friends, a real bore to be with. On the other hand, a worker is always enthusiastic about different happenings in school or at home, always occupied with school activities, family responsibilities, and great friends. This is your choice. Are you brave enough to be a leader? Or do you like to sit back and follow? About six years ago, I had a group of teen-agers who told me one day that they were bored to death at home and at school. I asked them if they had any hobbies. One of the boys, David, said, "I play guitar, but what's the use of playing when there isn't any-one to listen?" I agreed with him.

The group started a full combo. Dave began teaching the guys and myself how to play the guitar. Every day after school we practiced. We got together every lunchtime. Before you knew it, we had twelve guitar players, a drummer, and a bongo player. I taught them how to play the tambourine. We had two different kinds of tambourines, a bass and a regular. We had mass going with the Missa Bossa Nova. Be-fore the month was up, they asked if they could start having folk masses. The pastor was fantastic. We had to have two folk masses a week because the mass was so crowded. All because of these kids.

Before we realized it the first parish folk group was formed. Adults and children packed into church. These teen-agers set the parish afire with spirit and enthusiasm. What are you willing to give to make someone happy or to get some kind of project started in your parish, school, or community? All it takes is some soul-searching on your part. So study the good points about yourself. Your talents and your personality can spread and encourage others to spread good in turn. But we need someone to ignite the flame. Are you willing to strike the first match? In the past five years there has been a tremendous increase in the number of elderly citizens in our country. Have you ever thought that a group of you could bring some sunshine into their lives? How? Take turns shopping for them without looking for a tip in return. Or clean their apartments, or sit with them on a Sunday if they are alone. Take time to visit them, read to them, or write letters for them. I know of a group of teen-agers who call themselves the Sunshiners. They do exactly what I just described. It began as a community project in preparation for confirmation, and when they realized how useful they were and how they added to the senior citizens' lives, they decided to keep the group going. They began with seven members and now they have twenty. They do simple tasks that have a powerful impact on others.

Making an Effort

All you have to do is make the effort and the rest will fall into place. How about it? Talk it over with a couple of your friends. See if your group can come up with a first in your parish or community.

Did it ever occur to you that you were put on this earth to be there for others? That you weren't meant to be alone? That we need people in our lives? We cannot do it alone because God created us to work together in revealing God's love to others. We have a part in making our world a better place. Every one of us is challenged to be witnesses of our faith to all who come into our lives. We do this by being people of love, compassion, and justice to those we rub shoulders with daily. God calls on us to be genuinely concerned about others. Really caring for others, not only in words but by actions. We are responsible in many ways for each other. What do you do with your free class period or free time after school? My teen-age niece and a group of her girl friends took it upon themselves to ask the principal if they could do something more worthwhile during their study period. My niece looked on her study period as time for horsing around, and that made her realize how much time she and her friends had wasted. Have you ever thought that you could tutor little children? Once you get started, you really get a sense of satisfaction and fulfillment when you see their eyes brighten because you were able to explain a problem even better than their teacher.

How many wasted hours have you let go by? How do you feel about it? Have you reached out to someone lately? What are you to others? You camera buffs. Have you taken any pictures lately? Have you and your friends ever thought about putting a movie together about happenings in your school? It would be an exciting project to start using 8 mm cameras. Make a movie of all that goes on in one day in your school and ask to present it at the next PTA meeting or home-school association. You'll be providing information as well as entertainment for the evening. Think about it.

Being Important

Has it ever occurred to you how important you are to everyone around you? It is your responsibility to use whatever God-given talents you have to make a dream come true for someone, somewhere, at some time in your life. I challenge you to make an impossible dream become a reality for others. You have the power within you to do so. Pass the torch of hope to each other.

The goal is not to be perfect but rather to perfectly try. It's not impossible. And when I speak, it's through experience. We have to try. And things happen. You get surprised. All I ask is that you try, and that you really look at yourself as being valuable. You have lots to offer. And again, I challenge you to be you.

8. How to Express to Yourself How You Feel

Feeling Right

In the song "I've Gotta Be Me," there's a line that goes something like this: How can I be right for someone else when I'm not right for myself? How many times have you found yourself saying this? How do you know whether or not you're right for yourself? This is a difficult question because each one of us sets goals for ourselves at different levels. There aren't any rules regarding how high or low you rate on the scale. The important thing is that you realize that you have faults and weaknesses and strengths.

You are also made up of feelings. How you express these feelings will take a lifetime to figure out, but it doesn't mean you should forget about how to handle your feelings, yourself. You see you have to be right for yourself. You have to learn to deal with your feelings. In order to do this, you have to first recognize them and express them to yourself. If you wake up in the morning feeling mad at the world and you start taking it out on everyone who crosses your path that day, how do you expect others to react? If you wake up this way some morning, stop—and pause and reason out why. Did you have a spat with your parents or some of your friends the night before? You went to bed feeling resentful, with an I'll-show-them attitude. Therefore, when you woke up, you were prepared to fight a civil war all by yourself. Instead of ending your day that way, try to control this "rotten you" and channel the same energy to come up with the better you. If you make a habit out of thinking positively about yourself, a new you—the real you—can't help but begin to develop.

Feelings are tricky facets of our lives that sometimes overpower us to the point that we cannot see anything in front of us. Let me ask you this. How do you feel this very moment? How did you feel when you woke up this morning? Did you change any, get worse, or remain the same?

Think about your feelings right now, with me. Let's talk about what we can do together. OK? Let's go. First, let's take a day when you feel pressured or tense and everything bothers you. How do you handle it? Think why you're feeling this way. Did you let some of your assignments go until the last minute and then realize that you didn't have enough time to do them? You face a game or cheerleading tournament plus four projects. To avoid another day like this, why not begin to jot down a schedule for yourself to plan what project you will tackle on such a day? You will realize that the pressure is slowly coming off your shoulders.

When I was your age, I found myself pressured to the point that I began to feel miserable and "ratty" to others. Then I decided that I didn't like this side of me, and I did something constructive. I tackled my assignments right away, whether they were due immediately or in a month, and I began to find myself free to enjoy a lot of activities—sports, photography, the school newspaper. Things began to jell at home, too. My chores didn't seem so hard, for I set up a schedule for myself in tackling them. You know what the old song says: "When You're Smiling—the Whole World Smiles with You." People don't like to be around us when we wear a face so long that it touches the floor. You have too much to give.

Feeling Bad

How do you act when you wake up feeling sick? Do you fight it or accept it? When your muscles are sore and stiff after a round of exercise or a game, do you walk around as if it doesn't bother you because you want to prove to the girls that you are Mr. He-Man of the Year? I have a secret. You know, we women know that you are human and have days when your head feels like it is disconnected from your neck or weighs more than your barbells. Don't fight it. Accept your bad days with your good days.

When you girls have a bad day, how do you accept how you feel? Do you take it as part of your physical makeup and learn to roll with the punches, or are you ashamed because you cannot control how you feel? We all go through a whole range of feelings. It's the way we accept ourselves on these days that makes a difference in our attitude toward other things in life. So don't hide how you feel, learn to relax, and be yourself.

Blue Is OK

During my high school days there was a popular tune called "Blue Moon." We sang it every time we lost a game or felt out of it. Do you ever have blue days? Days when you're really down and don't know why? I used to chum around with a girl who sometimes used to say, "It's my blue day; I earned it, and I hope you'll respect it." We used to laugh at her and tell her how nuts she was. Before you knew it, she began to perk up and get into a happier frame of mind. But when I think about it, what she said made a lot of sense to me. For after what we go through simply coping with everyday pressures, we're entitled to a day to get out from under and gradually be ourselves again. In recovering from a blue day we can begin to appreciate all that surrounds us as well as the people who touch our lives.

When you get a blue day, accept it, for it's a part of life and a part of you.

Needing Support

What do you do when you're sad? Do you force yourself to be happy and go along with the gang? This is bad. You should feel free with your friends to express why you are sad. When I taught in Rochester, New York, there was a ninth-grade boy I noticed who was sad looking and somewhat pensive when walking alone. When the gang came around, he seemed to join in the fun. After a week of watching him, I approached him and asked him what was wrong. At first he gave me the usual response— "Nothing." I responded with, "Tell me another and I'll believe you."

After we laughed over what had just transpired, he began to cry. The reason for his sadness was rightful and heartfelt. He and his family had just gotten word that his mother had cancer and had six months to live.

He felt that, if he told the gang, they would look down on him because of how he was feeling. I told him that if they were real friends, they would support and help him and his family through the ordeal he had to face. I told him to take the risk and tell them, for this is when he really needed his friends. A couple of days later he came back to me grinning and thanking me. He told the gang, and to his surprise, they cried when they heard about his mother, for they too loved her. So you see, you don't necessarily have to remain alone in any situation that overwhelms you. What are friends for if you cannot share the important aspects of your life with them and expect some kind of help and support from them?

Moving On

What do you do when your best friend hurts you? Do you sulk or get angry? Do you ignore him or her or just forget it? Sometimes it's good to let out what's on your mind and to let your friend know exactly how you feel. I sometimes think we take each other for granted and at times have to be brought back to reality. Instead of stewing about it or griping to others, go to your friend and try to talk it over. It's so easy to cause pain and not be conscious of hurting others. So it's good to talk things over. I spoke with a tenth-grade girl who was upset because her boyfriend was spending more time with the guys after football practice than with her. This is normal. After a hard practice a guy usually wants to buy a soft drink and relax and talk over how things went at practice. Before you know it, time flies right by. He isn't thinking that you're waiting for him. He knows he'll be calling you shortly. So don't be too hard on him. Let him have time with his friends. This is healthy. Did you ever find yourself having a good day when everything seemed to fall into place? You're so happy you could burst with excitement. Then comes your grumpy friend who can't see anything nice or say anything nice about anything. Before you know it, you find yourself being dragged down, and your happy day becomes a dull one. Don't let that happen. If you're happy, keep that way. Be strong enough to pull your friend up with you. These happy days are few and far between, so hold onto them as much as you can.

Hidden Feelings

You see, we tend to hide or mask our feelings. We tend to hide our hurts, and we tend to diminish the precious happy moments because someone else isn't happy. Is this fair? Often we disguise our feelings. We find it easier at times to not be ourselves, for then we don't have to deal with our feelings. In plain English, we're running away from ourselves. What we find ourselves doing is acting our different roles because we don't want the authentic parts of our personalities to show. We do this because we're afraid of what the others will say.

The most common role we like to play is that of the clown. It seems to be the untouchable one. We're laughing on the outside and crying on the inside. By being a clown we kind of get permission to hide our feelings. We fail to look at our situations or the people we touch. How about when you take on the Mr. or Miss Cool mask. You become detached from any emotional ties. You put on the air that nothing bothers you. If your girl decides to go to the games with someone else, you're hurt, but you won't admit it. So you go around and tell others that you don't like her anyway.

We should begin to question our actions and ask what effect this type of masquerading has on us. Who are we kidding? You cannot play games with yourselves and others. If you have friends, you owe it to them to be real to them. Don't put on. Your friends are too important to you at this stage of the game. You see, if you're not a for-real person to your friends, gradually you'll begin to lose them. Your feelings are like blueprints of your personalities. People get to know you through these blueprints. So hang free and let go and be yourself. I know it's hard to share feelings. It is so different from sharing ideas and values; for feelings show the real you.

Sharing Feelings

Many unhappy homes exist today because you and your parents have failed to communicate your feelings. What was once a home becomes a house full of empty voices, for it's not a home until it's filled with love and honest communication.

Think About It

I would like you take the time to reflect on the the following questions:

When was I the happiest?

_____

_____

_____

When was I at peace with myself?

_____

_____

_____

When did I give of myself?

_____

_____

_____

_____

When did I show my true self through my feelings?

_____

_____

_____

_____

Only when you have answered these questions can you say in a proud way that you have accepted yourself and your life, and that you did it your way. I challenge you to live daily by the courage of your convictions and to be real to all who enter your life.

Keep the questions and your answers around. Read your answers a month or two from now. Answer the questions once more. Have you learned anything about yourself? These questions are a good guide to how happy you really are.

9. How to Express Feelings and Get a Positive Response

Being Honest

Do you trust yourself? You probably never thought about it until now. Has it ever occurred to you that the reason you're afraid to express your feelings is because you don't trust yourself? You're afraid of how they're going to come out. Each of us encounters a kaleidoscope of feelings, questions, and ideas within ourselves.

Try to take time right now to relax.

Lie down or sit in a comfortable position and play some soft music.

Think of some of your feelings or thoughts of the past week.

How did you express your feelings?

What was the reaction of others around you?

What ideas did you come up with?

Were they accepted or rejected?

Think hard first about the feelings you showed and the responses you received.

Were they positive or negative?

Think why they were either of the two.

Let's say you were in social studies class and the topic was politics. The class was shooting around different opinions about who would be the best man to be United States President. Inside, you were beginning to experience anger and frustration. What you were hearing seemed so stupid, and you couldn't believe your ears. Finally, you couldn't take it anymore, so you exploded. Your classmates were stunned, and at the end of the period everyone left without saying a word to you. You felt guilty because of how you reacted. Don't. You have a right to express how you feel. But it's the way you do it that can win you points.

Let's backtrack for a minute. Maybe what you should have done was to challenge your class to do more research on the person they thought was best for the position instead of using empty words and killing time in class. In doing that, you would have been channeling your anger creatively and constructively into a well-informed project and at the same time winning the admiration of your classmates. Learn to listen to your feelings and ideas, and allow them to be constructive and powerful in a positive way.

Knowing Feelings

Our personal makeup has potential that takes a lifetime to discover and nurture. It is a healthy challenge to you to be constantly aware of your feelings. Your feelings tell you something about what is happening in your life and gradually help you to begin planning for the future.

How many times have you shot off your mouth to your parents and in seconds wished you hadn't, for you saw a tear running down your mom's cheek? Try to think before you express how you feel. If, for example, your parents don't like the gang you're hanging around with, maybe it's because of what they've heard about the gang. You feel that what they've heard is untrue, and you feel not trusted by your parents. Instead of reacting in a tirade and hurting them and not accomplishing anything, tell them how you feel. Tell them that what they have heard is untrue, all image talk. Deep down the gang is great and has helped you. You feel hurt that they would think you would choose a bad bunch of friends. I guarantee, the more honest you are with your parents, the more the communication barrier can be broken. But the way you express how you feel will determine what kind of response you will get.

Listening to Feelings

If you fail to listen to your inner self, you begin to lessen the process of growing toward a fully alive self. If you trust your inner self you can acknowledge what has happened to you in the past. You can begin to learn from your experiences and move forward toward a healthful way of life. You can also begin to affirm your personal worth and goodness. The truth is, you are great. But you have to convince yourself of this truth and not let anyone change your mind.

Life is not a series of games where you win or lose. It is a wealth of discoveries that allow you to grow in a mature way. If you doubt this, think of Jesus' life. He affirmed us by choosing to be one of us. I'm sure that while he was growing up, he had the same questions, feelings, ideas, and decisions to make that you and I have. When he was twelve he ran away to listen to the priests in the temple. Remember what he put his parents through? The anxiety of not knowing where he was or whether he was alive or dead. When they did find him, he was sitting listening and sharing with the priests and Joseph reproached him, saying, "Do you realize what worry you have caused us?" He didn't respond to that, but he said, "I must be about my Father's business." I am sure that he realized how much he had hurt his parents, yet he also knew no other way to explain what happened. Finally, he went quietly home with them.

Checking Yourself

How many times have you caused unnecessary pain because you did not check yourself? If you were to express or explain your relationship with your parents and brothers and sisters, what songs could you use to best describe it?

_____

_____

_____

_____

_____

_____

_____

_____

Being Afraid

Most of our anger is fear. How we react to various situations is often colored by what we are afraid of. The emotional patterns that we develop now are part of growing up and maturing. So you shouldn't be ashamed of the way you react and respond to things. We get the word *emotion* from the Latin *emovere* which means "to move out." Emotions have to be expressed somehow, some way. They have to leave our bodies so they won't be pent up or they might even cause us to be ill (in a state of dis-ease) or ill at ease with ourselves and others.

If you love someone, don't be afraid to say so. Even if you think it's "puppy love." Listen, gang, we all love someone at one time or another. We make friends and develop friendships that may last a lifetime. Loving is the risk you have to take. I know you're afraid to be hurt. It's natural. I've been hurt a lot, and at one point in my life I refused to share myself with others. That was the worst year in my life. I felt no warmth and almost froze to death without the warmth of a friend saying how much she or he cared.

You are at an age when you are developing friendships, and it's possible that you'll be hurt, at times crushed. Don't stop loving and reaching out. You need people to help you along your path of life. You have a right to be loved and accepted by your classmates. You have the right to express yourself to others. Keep in mind that all your emotions are in some way related to your body and affect your body.

For example, when you are insulted, you cannot help feeling angry. The physical things you feel (warm face, knots in your stomach, blurry vision, sweating, and so on) cannot be controlled, but you can respond in a much milder way than what you are feeling. You have no control over what sets you off, but you do have control over how you are going to express what you feel at a given moment. You don't have to react automatically.

Discovering

How many of us have realized the importance of feelings in our lives? The integral part they play in our relationships with others and also how they help us to understand ourselves better? I urge you to take time out once in a while to listen to your inner promptings and to learn what a unique individual you are. You have to get in touch with your feelings before others can begin to understand you. You are important enough to know and understand; give others a chance to discover you and see for themselves how great you are. Let go and be yourself for those of us who love you.

Exercises to Get in Touch

Here are ten exercises to help you get in touch with your feelings so that you may take actions that help you become more you and at ease with others.

One

If you were given a million dollars to form a group that would bring joy to someone, get someone out of a rut, or be of service:

   a) What will you call the group? _____

_____

_____

   b) What will your group do? ("Sunshiners" bring sunshine to the elderly by shopping, writing letters, reading to them, etc.) _____

_____

_____

_____

_____

_____

_____

Two

When I talk about people being different, I mean the different qualities of personality that we deal with each day. Think of some of the people in your life and place them according to the seasons of the year.

a) **Fall type people** are those with varied talents and gifts and vibrant with love and joy.

b) **Winter type people** are those who strip themselves of selfishness like the barren land in order to "be" for others and give of themselves to others in need.

c) **Spring type people** are those who are not afraid of new challenges and tasks. They are igniters of new life.

d) **Summer type people** are those who are able to recreate people into being at ease with themselves or others, they are easy to talk to, good listeners.

Spring People

Summer People

Fall People

Winter People

Three

Keep a journal entitled *Me, Myself, and I*, and jot down once a week how someone made God or love real to you that particular week. Be specific about the person and the incident. For example, you were put down by a supposed friend and word of it came back to you. You were hurt. Another person came into your life and, without knowing what had just happened to you, complimented some quality about you. You gave an excellent speech in English class.

Journal page

a) **Today I felt love because** _____

_____

_____

_____

_____

b) Today I saw love when _____

_____

_____

c) When I was hurt _____

_____

d) I know someone loves me when _____

_____

_____

e) I know I am loved because _____

_____

_____

_____

_____

Four

You have to be yourself and no one else in order to be at ease with yourself and comfortable with others. Jot down ten things you expect from yourself in order to be "real." For example: I want to be able to face myself honestly when I do something wrong.

The real me is . . .

1. _____

2. _____

3. _____

4. _____

5. _____

6. _____

7. _____

8. _____

9. _____

10. _____

Five

When we talk about friendship, we think of certain qualities in a friend that we admire. Write ten good points or qualities that you admire in your friend and make a collage depicting those qualities.

A good friend is . . .

1. _____

2. _____

3. _____

4. _____

5. _____

6. _____

7. _____

8. _____

9. _____

10. _____

A good friend does . . .

1. _____

2. _____

3. _____

4. _____

5. _____

6. _____

7. _____

8. _____

9. _____

10. _____

Six

Write in your own words how you tuned Christ into your life. Illustrate what you wrote by any art form (collage, painting, drawing, etc.).

I found Christ in

_____

_____

_____

_____

_____

_____

_____

Seven

Describe your relationship with your family by using a popular song on the market (e.g., "Leaving on a Jet Plane"). Be able to explain your feelings about the song to your listeners.

The song _____ describes my family life because . . .

_____

_____

_____

_____

_____

_____

Eight

When you think of your gang or the friends you pal around with, you think of a support group. Write ten different ways your gang supports and encourages you.

1. _____

2. _____

3. _____

4. _____

5. _____

6. _____

7. _____

8. _____

9. _____

10. _____

Nine

Do you believe that people who need people are the luckiest people in the world? Show why you agree or disagree.

People who need people are (not) the luckiest people because . . .

_____

_____

_____

_____

_____

_____

_____

_____

_____

_____

_____

Ten

Are you convinced that you are important? Let's see. Jot down names of everyone you know beginning with family, relatives, friends, schoolmates, and people in your neighborhood. Put each name on a three-inch strip of paper and staple them together forming a chain. See how many lives you've touched already? Are you important?

— — — — — — — — — — — —

— — — — — — — — — — — —

— — — — — — — — — — — —

— — — — — — — — — — — —

— — — — — — — — — — — —

— — — — — — — — — — — —

— — — — — — — — — — — —

— — — — — — — — — — — 4C